Moments in His Presence

40 DAYS OF INTIMATE PURSUIT

Dawn Hill

To my wonderful husband, Nicholas.
Thank you for loving me through
every season. To Annie Edwards,
thank you for designing this beautiful
book cover, and for being a dear
friend. Most importantly, thank You,
Jesus, for loving me beyond my own
comprehension and boundaries. Your
Presence has forever wrecked me.

Introduction

Lovesick. As I read through my journal, reminiscing on private moments with God, I notice myself using the word lovesick several times. This one word truly describes the depths of my desire for the Lord. Fifteen years ago, I made the most important decision of my life. I chose to answer His voice as He called out to me. I was a broken young woman full of rejection and insecurity, and in one moment, Jesus began a transformation in me as I asked him to make His home inside of me.

The journey has not always been comfortable or easy. Dying to self is neither comfortable nor easy, but having Him, every bit of Him, means more to me than any comfort ever could. What you hold in your hands is a portion of a personal treasure. It is a taste of an ongoing conversation between the Father and His daughter, the Bridegroom and His bride, as Holy Spirit bellows through every crevice of my being. I selected entries from a journal I have faithfully kept for the past four and a half years to share with you in this devotional. These are the entries of a lovesick scribe.

I chose forty days because forty is a significant number in the Bible. Forty is a number signifying testing and trying. Jesus fasted for forty days and forty nights in the wilderness. The twelve spies investigated the Promised Land for forty days. Goliath taunted the Israelites for forty days, and Moses was on Mount Sinai for forty days and forty nights. These are but a few of many examples from Scripture regarding the significance of forty. Despite it being a time of testing and trying, something significant transpired after each event.

Jesus officially began His ministry. A generation of Israelites was cut off from inheriting the Promised Land due to disobedience. A shepherd boy named David became a giant slayer, and Moses received the instruction of the Lord for God's people. The number forty may hold testing, but on the other side of that testing is tremendous breakthrough, pending personal stewardship of that time.

Forty is also the number of weeks for an average human pregnancy. I carried our daughter full term, and I remember the changes that took place both in my body and in her body during those forty weeks. There were moments of testing, trying and stretching, but out of that time came the birth of a beautiful and amazing child.

The Lord desires to birth something in you from this devotional. He desires to fertilize your very being with passion, transparency, and holiness so that pure intimacy with Christ is birthed. There are days in this devotional that may test you and stretch you, but if you steward it well, something greater awaits you on the other side. Jesus desires to commune with you so that as you behold His glory as in a mirror, you will be transformed into His image with intensifying glory, which only comes from the Lord who is the Spirit (2 Corinthians 3:18).

As you go on this journey of intimacy with Christ, I encourage you to do the following each day:

- get alone with God in a quiet place
- worship the Lord and invite Holy Spirit to speak to you during this time
- meditate on what He is saying to you through His Word and the devotional
- write down what God is sharing with you on the area provided after each day
- pray out loud to Jesus, whether you recite the daily prayer provided, or you pray using your own words
- Receive communion daily (This is a powerful facet of our relationship with Christ. I have provided a section at the end of this devotional for receiving personal communion along with Scriptures to meditate on as you receive communion.)

I pray this devotional leaves you wanting more, more of Christ and more of His Presence. May you understand that Heavenly Father longs to take you into His arms and embrace you as His child. If you are not doing so already, I pray this ignites a passion within you to journal with God for yourself. He is always speaking to us, and He loves to share His heart with us. At the end of this forty days, I pray the Lord births such intimacy within you that all else pales in comparison to Him. Enjoy the journey. There is nothing like His love.

-Dawn Hill, *The Lovesick Scribe*

LET HIM KISS ME WITH THE KISSES OF HIS MOUTH! FOR YOUR LOVE IS BETTER THAN WINE; YOUR ANOINTING OILS ARE FRAGRANT; YOUR NAME IS OIL POURED OUT; THERE VIRGINS LOVE YOU. DRAW ME AFTER YOU; LET US RUN. THE KING HAS BROUGHT ME INTO HIS CHAMBERS. SONG OF SOLOMON 1:2–4

Table of Contents

My 40-Day Journey

Let the Journey begin

Day 1

The Call of Deep Intimacy

"I feel You all around me. Your Presence is insatiable to me. Your touch is beyond words and beyond understanding to my flesh, but my spirit knows you well. There can be no other for me but You, my LORD. The Lover of my soul has captured my heart, and He has made it His home. I think of Song of Solomon when it says, "I am a garden enclosed". I am Your resting place. I want more of You. I am desperate for Your Presence and Your love. This romance is unlike any I have ever known. This love is reserved only for You, Jesus. I have given myself to You, and I am Yours forever. I love You, beyond words, beyond my own comprehension, beyond eternity. You truly are my everything. Thank You for Your unfailing love, Your rich grace upon my life and Your abundant favor."
Journal Entry February 12, 2013

SONG OF SOLOMON 4:11–12, 5:8

PRAYER:
Jesus, help me to love You more deeply every day. Increase my desire for more of You. Remind me throughout the day that You desire to spend time with me and to share Your heart with me. Possess me with a heart of gratitude before You in every aspect of my life. Holy Spirit, I am Your resting place. I want to create a habitation where You will remain. Create a desperation and a hunger in me for Your Presence.

I hear Him saying,

_____

_____

_____

_____

_____

_____

_____

_____

_____

_____

_____

_____

_____

_____

_____

_____

_____

_____

Day 2

Fear Is Not My Inheritance

I hear Him say, "Do not be afraid. Do not fear or operate in fear of any kind. I am still your God. I hear you when you pray. Continue to lift up prayers to My throne. I hear the cry of the remnant, My remnant. The bride is dripping with oil. Let it flow out. Saturate the atmosphere with prayer and worship. Do not back down. Do not give up. Remain faithful to Me. I am always faithful to you."
Journal Entry November 6, 2012

JOSHUA 1:9, 2 TIMOTHY 1:7

PRAYER:
Father, I thank You for Your Word, and I thank You that fear is not my inheritance. Your Word is full of declarations to not be afraid, and to remember that You are with me wherever I go. I declare that boldness in You is my inheritance. I break off fear in my life, and I say that I am as a bold as a lion because I belong to You. Jesus, speak to me and reveal to me what You are praying in heaven before the throne. Increase my desire to pray and to intercede. Let my life drip with Your anointing, and have Your perfect way in me.

I hear Him saying,

_____

_____

_____

_____

_____

_____

_____

_____

_____

_____

_____

_____

_____

_____

_____

_____

_____

Day 3

The Perfect Hiding Place

"My life is hidden in Christ with God. It is not my ministry, but it is His ministry because to be truly in Him means that I am not seen or at the forefront. I am His yielded vessel, and I am not my own. I have relinquished the right to my ways because my life is hidden in Christ with God. LORD, help me to remember this every moment of every day. Help me to set my mind on things above and not on this earth. I want to die to myself and truly live hidden in You."
Journal Entry October 20, 2013

COLOSSIANS 3:3, EPHESIANS 2:4–7

PRAYER:
Father, I long to put under the drive for ambition and self-promotion so that I can glorify You. I want to know You and to find contentment in knowing that my true identity is found in You, Jesus. Holy Spirit, search every part of me and purify my motives and intentions. Have Your way in my life and let me always be quick to lift Your name above my own. I yield to Your plans and Your voice, and I delight being hidden in Your Presence.

I hear Him saying,

_____

_____

_____

_____

_____

_____

_____

_____

_____

_____

_____

_____

_____

_____

_____

_____

_____

Day 4

Releasing His Fiery Boldness

I hear Him say, "You are beautiful. Whenever I look at you, I see My Son. I see Myself. You are holding back. There is a well, a depth in you I long to excavate and release. Do not concern yourself with what people think of you. Fire is to be released from your belly and uttered from your tongue. Keep pressing. Pay no attention to naysayers. Do not change your profession, not even a little. Remain bold. I did not create you to be warm like an ember. I created you to be hot like a raging fire. Let me burn out hindrances. The veil is consumed. Dwell in My Presence. Release it all to Me. "
Journal Entry June 28, 2013

PROVERBS 28:1, ACTS 4:23–31

PRAYER:
Father, I thank You for freedom from man's opinion and that my worth is found in You. Stir up the boldness of Your Holy Spirit on the inside of me. I want to release a mighty roar for You. I want to be consumed with passion for You. Burn out every hindrance that would keep me from Your Presence. I come boldly before Your throne, and I seek You above all things, Jesus.

I hear Him saying,

_____

_____

_____

_____

_____

_____

_____

_____

_____

_____

_____

_____

_____

_____

_____

_____

Day 5

Let His Virtue Flow Through Me

I hear Him say, "My glory is filling My temple, My vessels. My people are not only meant to carry My glory, but they are to dispense My glory. The train of My robe holds virtue, and power is to be released from it. That is why I fill My bride with it. Virtue and power are to flow out of My bride. The whole earth is full of My glory. Will you release it? Will you dispense it? Just as Isaiah was a living sacrifice branded by My fire, I also desire you to be a holy living sacrifice unto Me."
Journal Entry January 26, 2014

ISAIAH 6, MARK 5:25-34

PRAYER:
Father, I desire to be a vessel of glory for Your Kingdom. I desire not only to house Your glory, Your virtue, and Your power, but I desire to release Your glory to those I come in contact. Heighten my sensitivity to Your Presence. As I lay myself upon Your altar as a living sacrifice, let all that You are fill my being and consume me with passion for You and for the desires of Your heart. You want to see people saved, healed, delivered and set free by Your power. Let that same virtue found in the hem of Your garment flow through me freely and without any hindrance to those who need Your touch, Jesus.

I hear Him saying,

_____

_____

_____

_____

_____

_____

_____

_____

_____

_____

_____

_____

_____

_____

_____

_____

Day 6

Overtake Me, Lord

"God, the longing of my heart is that you would reveal Yourself fully to me. I have allowed things to hinder me, and I have allowed my flesh to be in control at times, but I desire that You, Holy Spirit, would overtake me. I repeatedly said this morning as I wept in Your Presence, "I yield myself to You, God." Consume me. Inhabit me. I succumb to You and to Your will. All I want is You. I will pay the price to see Your glory."
Journal Entry March 25, 2013

JOHN 14:18–21, JOHN 17:20–26

PRAYER:
Jesus, my heart aches to know You more. My spirit is willing, but my flesh is weak at times. I repent of those times when I have placed fleshly desires over the desire to pursue You. I lay aside distractions and those things which keep me from giving my all to You. I know You desire me, and I want to be overtaken by You. I have counted the cost, and You are worth it all to Me, LORD. Search me, God and reveal to me the things that need to be stripped from my life so that nothing stands between us.

I hear Him saying,

Day 7

I Am Not Forgotten

I hear Him say, "You must want Me more than you want the calling. Permit me to forge you and to mold you. There is a process for you to go through before you can be released. I know you feel forgotten, but I have not forgotten you. This time is uncomfortable, but such as it is when I am reshaping and refining you in My fire. Do not despise this time because if you will remain in this season, you will come out transformed and ready to go forth as a mighty weapon. The enemy will fight, and you will want to give up, but know that I AM with you. You are not forgotten, not by Me. You are always in My sight. Don't give up. I will never give up on you. You cannot measure the depth of My love for you."
Journal Entry August 16, 2015

ISAIAH 49:14–16, 1 CHRONICLES 28:20

PRAYER:
I am so thankful for Your love, Father. You are faithful and good, and I am so thankful to You. No matter how I feel or what I face, You love me. You have never forgotten me. You know me by name. I refuse to give up on the plans and purposes you have ordained for my life. Forge me in Your fire, and refine my very being so that Your reflection comes forth. I place all my trust in You, Jesus.

I hear Him saying,

_____

_____

_____

_____

_____

_____

_____

_____

_____

_____

_____

_____

_____

_____

_____

_____

Day 8

I Submit To His Process

I hear Him say, "Build an altar on the threshing floor. Do not concern yourself with trying to remove the chaff. I will do that when you bring yourself as a sacrifice. As you do, My fire, My wind, and My breath shall remove the chaff. You may feel crushed, but you are not defeated. Give into Me and not this world. Build an altar in your threshing floor, and worship Me regardless of flaws, hindrances, and short comings. When people do not like you or even hate you, rest in knowing that I love you. I will help you. Trust in Me."
Journal Entry June 29, 2014

1 CHRONICLES 21:18–28, RUTH 3:2–14

PRAYER:
Heavenly Father, I lay myself in the threshing floor, and I submit to the process of unveiling the wheat from the chaff. I know that this process will crush things out of me, but it is necessary in my life. Separate me from those things that delay Your harvest in my life. Breathe on me, Holy Spirit, and blow away the chaff during this process. I come to You, my Bridegroom and I lay myself at Your feet. I will not despise the process because it means drawing closer to You.

I hear Him saying,

_____

_____

_____

_____

_____

_____

_____

_____

_____

_____

_____

_____

_____

_____

_____

_____

Day 9

His Presence Is Everything

"I will worship You with every ounce of worship that is in me. I will break myself at Your feet and allow the fragrance of adoration and worship to saturate Your Throne. I yield myself to You, fully and completely. I will dwell in Your chambers, and I will inhabit Your secret place. Your face is what I long to see. Your breath is what I long to feel within my spirit. Your touch is precious. It thrills me and it comforts me. Your Presence is everything to me, Abba. My Jesus, My Jesus. My great Love. My Husband, My Bridegroom. How I love you."

Journal Entry July 14, 2013

PSALM 27:4,8, SONG OF SOLOMON 2:8–17

PRAYER:
Jesus, I long to draw closer to You. I desire intimacy with You. My heart is thankful, knowing that when I come to meet with You, You are there to meet with me. I will make a lifestyle of seeking You daily. I invite Your Presence to invade every part of my being. Interrupt my schedule, and consume me with passion for the secret place. Let the cry of my heart be to know You and to be a faithful bride to You, Jesus. Nothing compares to Your Presence.

I hear Him saying,

_____

_____

_____

_____

_____

_____

_____

_____

_____

_____

_____

_____

_____

_____

_____

_____

Day 10

The God Of Refreshing

I hear Him say, "This is My desire, that My children would walk in My fullness. Partiality is intolerable. I must have it all. My dwelling place is not adorned with dry and dead spaces, but My dwelling place is full of life, and a river flows where I am found. The dams and barges of religion must be removed so that My anointing can flow freely, so waters can penetrate every area, all the way to the very core of My habitation in you. Begin to cry out to the dry places of My people, and declare that the rain is coming. A downpour is headed straight for the depths of My bride. The dust that has collected to blind My people will cease and settle. It will be overtaken by Me. There is nothing dry in My Presence. I long for life to abound in you and through you."

Journal Entry March 7, 2013

ISAIAH 18:43, JOHN 7:37–39

PRAYER:

Father, invade the dry places within me. Holy Spirit, flood every part of me. I repent of times I have remained dry while You have invited me to have my riverbanks overflowing with Your anointing. Open my eyes to see, and clear the dust from my field of vision. I come alive in You, Jesus. My desire is beyond religion. I desire relationship with You. Make me a change agent spilling over with Your Living water.

I hear Him saying,

_____

_____

_____

_____

_____

_____

_____

_____

_____

_____

_____

_____

_____

_____

_____

Day 11

The Weight Of His Glory

I hear Him say, "The full weight of My glory is for those who seek My face. They will shine with My countenance and be forever changed by My everlasting love for them. I have illuminated the path with My Word and My Spirit. Walk on this path into My Presence. Come, spotless bride, I wait for you. Since I shined on the face of Moses under a former covenant, how much more will I shine on you and through you? Turn your face to the One Who knows you and longs to be reflected through you. I wait for you."

Journal Entry March 28, 2013

2 CORINTHIANS 3:7-18, HAGGAI 2:9

PRAYER:
Father, You have told me to seek Your face, and I respond by seeking Your face. I desire for Your countenance to rest upon me, and for Your Light to radiate from every part of my life. Come and have Your perfect way in me, LORD. I am so thankful to have the promise of a better covenant. Let me not take it for granted what You desire to do in me and through me. I am Yours.

I hear Him saying,

_____

_____

_____

_____

_____

_____

_____

_____

_____

_____

_____

_____

_____

_____

_____

_____

Day 12

My Trust Is In Him

"I trust You, God and this is my declaration. I will serve You every day. I will die to myself and live for You and You alone. I bend to Your will, and I seek You with everything I have. I want You, and I desire for You to be glorified through my life. So fill me up with Your robe, the hem of Your train. Let Your oil drip from this life. Find me faithful, and let Your glory shine on me and through me. I love You, Jesus. Touch the coal to my lips, and let my life be a sweet incense before Your Throne."

Journal Entry January 20, 2014

PSALM 9:10, PSALM 33:20–22, ISAIAH 12:2

PRAYER:
Jesus, the greatest thing I can do with this life is to live it for You. When I truly know You, Your nature will pour out of me. Use me to minister Your love and Your healing power to others. I trust that when You lead me to minister to those in need, You will show up. You are never absent. Teach me to be faithful and to always place my trust in You, no matter the situation.

I hear Him saying,

_____

_____

_____

_____

_____

_____

_____

_____

_____

_____

_____

_____

_____

_____

_____

_____

_____

Day 13

A Mansion Will Not Satisfy Me

I asked the Father this morning if instead of a mansion in heaven, I could dwell at His feet in His Throne Room. I wept as I thought of spending an eternity at His feet, worshiping Him and exalting His Name. We were created to worship Him. My heart aches to be close to Him, and yet He is closer than my skin. I would give up all other rooms to dwell in the secret place forever. My desire is to remain in the inner chamber with Him and to gaze upon His beauty. A mansion just won't do. I want to dwell in the Throne Room.
Journal Entry January 29, 2017

PSALM 84:10, REVELATION 4

PRAYER:
My God, the greatest position I could ever attain is postured at Your feet. I am in awe of Your splendor and Your beauty. Intensify a passion in me to dwell in the secret place with You. I was not made for the outer courts. I was made to be close to You. In Your Presence, I find protection, provision and peace, but even greater than these things are the moments of communion with You. You are the One I desire above all things. I fix my eyes on You, Jesus.

I hear Him saying,

_____

_____

_____

_____

_____

_____

_____

_____

_____

_____

_____

_____

_____

_____

_____

Day 14

Dreaming With God

I hear Him say, "I withhold nothing good from you. It is My delight to give you My promises. Dream on, My child. When you ask Me, I am willing to bestow every promise upon you. Only believe. You have asked Me for things right now, and I am willing to do what you have asked by faith. What you desire you can have because it is according to My Word. What you envision can come to pass. Dream on, dream big. I am willing."
Journal Entry September 27, 2015

PSALM 20:4–5, EPHESIANS 3:20–21

PRAYER:
Father, I choose to dream big! You have placed desires on the inside of me that line up with Your Word, and they are dreams from Your heart to mine. I will not place limitations on what You can do in my life. When I dream big, I am dreaming Your dreams, and I activate my faith to believe for the extraordinary. Thank You for speaking to me in my dreams and for revealing things by Your Spirit. I will be sensitive to Your prompting, and I will obey Your call to dream beyond my comfort zone.

I hear Him saying,

_____

_____

_____

_____

_____

_____

_____

_____

_____

_____

_____

_____

_____

_____

_____

Day 15

Strip Off The Old Garments

I hear Him say, "Strip off the old garments, the garments of death and despair, and put on My garment of praise. I long for people to desire the garments I have reserved for them. I long to see them come out from the dead places and into My glorious light. Listen to My voice! I am calling them out of the tombs and out of the dead places into life and life more abundantly."
Journal Entry January 9, 2015

ISAIAH 61:3, JOHN 11:38–44

PRAYER:
Jesus, I hear Your voice to come out of the place of death and despair, the place of heaviness and unrest. You desire for me to adorn a garment of praise and joy. When I do that, I come alive in You. As You call my name, I am coming out of the dead and dry places, and I am exchanging my apparel. Your garments remove the decay of yesterday. I am dancing out of my grave clothes and into Your Presence. Thank You, LORD, for Your love and for Your abundant life that resurrects, restores and rejuvenates.

I hear Him saying,

_____

_____

_____

_____

_____

_____

_____

_____

_____

_____

_____

_____

_____

_____

_____

Day 16

Running Into His Presence

I hear Him say, "I desire those who will run into My bed chamber before they will desire the platform. I desire those who will be content with the echoes of My heart in the prayer closet and the secret place before they desire the sound of their own voice on a microphone. When hunger for Me is released, heaven responds and heaven flows. The cloud of glory is coming in to those areas where hunger rises like a giant tidal wave. As this tidal wave of desperation rises and crests toward My throne, My glory comes crashing down. As My glory comes, My people will posture their hearts and themselves in response to My glory."
Journal Entry August 9, 2015

2 CHRONICLES 7:1–3, MATTHEW 5:6–8

PRAYER:
My Jesus, my entire being cries out to be with You and to know You more. Let the desires of my heart be pure. Intimacy is what You desire, and that is the cry of my soul as I pursue You. Let the weight of Your glory rest upon my life as I lay myself before You, God. Transform me in Your glory. Let Your Weighty Presence crash over me and consume me. I come running into secret place because there is no better place to be than with You.

I hear Him saying,

_____

_____

_____

_____

_____

_____

_____

_____

_____

_____

_____

_____

_____

_____

_____

_____

Day 17

Consecration For The Bride

I hear Him say, "The time of fasting and consecration is here. I long to purge My vessels and prepare them to manifest the fullness of what is coming. I must remain the tip of the spear, piercing to the joints, marrow and hearts of My people. It must be My Words and My heart released over people. Grandiose words without My power will not penetrate the depths of My bride. This is not a movement nor is it another visitation, but it is a cohabitation cemented in My love. Obedience to this fasting and consecration will cause an evacuation of the impervious."

Journal Entry July 2, 2013

JOEL 2:12–17, HEBREWS 10:19–23

PRAYER:
Father, I answer the call of Your heart to come closer to You by forsaking the desires of my flesh. You are calling me to be set apart for You and to be a laid down lover. I will live a lifestyle of fasting for my Bridegroom. Guide me, Holy Spirit, to fast as You lead. I long for Your return and for You to be exalted through me. I refuse to lose my sharp edge by not meditating on and professing Your Word, God. Let me dispense Your love, Your Presence, and Your truth as I live a consecrated life unto You, Jesus.

I hear Him saying,

_____

_____

_____

_____

_____

_____

_____

_____

_____

_____

_____

_____

_____

_____

_____

_____

Day 18

I Want To Know You

"I held my Father's hand last night. We walked through a field full of wheat. We sat on a hillside, His arms wrapped around me. I want to know You, God. I want to know Your heart and look into Your eyes of fire. I want to be perpetually enamored by Your splendor and majesty. I want to spend my life at Your feet, to stand at the altar with You and to experience again and again Your kisses, sweet Jesus. You are my beloved Bridegroom, the one my soul cries out to behold in the secret chambers. You have captivated my heart. Don't ever let it go, LORD. I want to know You. I want to gaze at You in utter amazement and to love You with reckless abandon. My very being wants to know You."
Journal Entry September 28, 2013

PHILIPPIANS 3:10–12, PSALM 63:1–8

PRAYER:

I want to know You, Father. I am Your child, and You long to embrace me as Your own. You delight in me, and You love when I come to You in the quiet times. I want to know You, Jesus. I want to romance You and to love You passionately. I am Yours, and You are mine. I want to know You, Holy Spirit, and to be a resting place for Your Presence to dwell. Find me as a faithful child, bride, and holy tabernacle.

I hear Him saying,

_____

_____

_____

_____

_____

_____

_____

_____

_____

_____

_____

_____

_____

_____

_____

_____

Day 19

The Vision To Be Broken

I hear Him say, "Vision is returning to My people. The scales are falling off, and those who will see with My eyes will walk in My fullness. The key to this level of vision will be a love flowing from My throne room, a love which sees past the surface and the natural, a love penetrating the spirit and piercing the heart of My children to love with purity and compassion. With My vision, you will see people differently. A brokenness must exist in your heart to love this way. This brokenness comes with the shattering of a heart of stone hardened by the world and circumstances. A hardened heart cannot beat with the rhythm of heaven. Brokenness brings love, and love brings the flood of My anointing."

Journal Entry November 22, 2012

PSALM 51:10–12,15–17, ACTS 9:17–18

PRAYER:
Let the scales fall from my spiritual eyes, LORD. I want to see as You see and love as You love. I repent for blindness and hardness of heart. Soften my heart where stone has resided and a heartbeat has been void. I want the heartbeat of my Father. Write Your name and Your Word upon my heart, and renew a right spirit in me. Invade my being with a brokenness for people and for the things that break Your heart.

I hear Him saying,

_____

_____

_____

_____

_____

_____

_____

_____

_____

_____

_____

_____

_____

_____

_____

_____

Day 20

A Spotless Bride

I hear Him say, "I alone cleanse My bride. I remove her stains and renew her garments. There is no veil to remove from My spotless bride. I see her and receive her as My own. My pure bride seeks Me and no other. She seeks no title nor position because My pure bride understands that her greatest position is with the Bridegroom, hidden in Jesus...I will not compete with others for authority. My Kingdom is unshakeable. If My people would fully yield to Me, I would consume them, causing them to burn brighter than the sun. I am jealous to consume My bride and for her passion to be only for Me."

Journal Entry October 20, 2013

ISAIAH 54:4–5, EPHESIANS 5:25–27

PRAYER:

Jesus, it is by Your Blood that I am transformed and eternally cleansed. Your Blood and Your sacrifice has removed the stains from the bridal garments. I submit to Your will every day, and I ask that You purify every part of my life. I will give my affection to no other but You, Jesus. I yield to You and to Your ways. Consume me, LORD. I desire to be fully one with You and to be the wife that You redeemed.

I hear Him saying,

_____

_____

_____

_____

_____

_____

_____

_____

_____

_____

_____

_____

_____

_____

_____

_____

Day 21

Faith and Glory

I hear Him say, "Faith requires movement and action. There is a measure of faith found in Me which cannot be measured or even comprehended, unless self is lost and reason of man is forsaken. People want glory, but many do not want My glory. Do not be deceived. Coming into My glory will cost you. Yes, I paid the price as Your High Priest for salvation, healing, redemption, provision and protection, but as a priest of a royal priesthood, much is asked of My bride. If priests under the Old Covenant were held to a higher standard to even breathe in My Presence, what makes you think a higher standard will not be asked of you? The priest always came with a sacrifice to offer. Your sacrifice is you, yielding unto Me and allowing the fire to burn with purity and with full intensity."

Journal Entry June 18, 2013

HEBREWS 11, 1 PETER 2:4–5

PRAYER:

Jesus, I have counted the cost, and I choose to come after You. You said to be holy because You are holy. I will not be moved by circumstances, but rather by faith. I will not just talk about faith, but I will put action to my profession of faith. Let Your fire consume me and refine me. Find me full of faith and overflowing with Your glory.

I hear Him saying,

_____

_____

_____

_____

_____

_____

_____

_____

_____

_____

_____

_____

_____

_____

_____

Day 22

No Room For Offense

I hear Him say, "See to it that no offense resides or lodges within your spirit. The heart will receive it freely, and it will attempt to engraft itself into your spirit. It is a weed cloaking itself with self-righteousness, but it is diseased, and it chokes out life. It will distract you, and there is no time for distractions. Permit people to say things without defending yourself. Chase after Me and seek Me. This offense will act as a detour, if you permit it. It will close off the path to go deeper into My Presence. Remove this distraction. Repent of offense and release it. Kill it with blessings and the Word. The deeper you go in Me, the stronger attacks will be, but rest in Me. I am with you. Make no time for offense in your life."

Journal Entry July 21, 2013

LUKE 17:1–4, JAMES 3:9–11

PRAYER:
Father, I welcome Your Living water to flow through me. I refuse to pollute my spirit with the bitter waters of offense. Search me and reveal to me if there is any offense in me, Holy Spirit. Close off these streams in me. I choose forgiveness, even to those who do not ask for it, and I refuse to give the enemy a foothold in my life with offense or resentment.

I hear Him saying,

_____

_____

_____

_____

_____

_____

_____

_____

_____

_____

_____

_____

_____

_____

_____

_____

Day 23

Abiding In The Radical

I hear Him say, "I am the Vine, and you are the branch. Apart from Me, you can do nothing. Radical ones, those arising from the Root, must remain in Me. If forgiveness and compassion are lacking for those who kill you and hate you, then you are not of Me. You do not battle against flesh and blood, but against principalities and powers. Your enlistment into My army is to battle and confront the kingdom of darkness, not man. Let the cries for your enemies arise. Let compassion arise for those who kill My children because without compassion to open doors for salvation, those people will be eternally separated from me. Where is My bride's heart?"
Journal Entry February 22, 2015

JOHN 15:1–9, MATTHEW 5:43–48

PRAYER:
Jesus, thank You for Your unconditional love and for teaching me how to love others, no matter how they may treat me. I want to abide in You, and as an abider, I know that I am to emanate Your nature. Overwhelm me with compassion for those who would persecute me and curse me. Give me Your eyes to see, LORD, and a passion to intercede for them as You would. I declare radical encounters with Your Presence to transform them and to rescue them from darkness.

I hear Him saying,

_____

_____

_____

_____

_____

_____

_____

_____

_____

_____

_____

_____

_____

_____

_____

Day 24

An Audience Of One

I hear Him say, "If you could see what is highlighted and brought to light in heaven, you would see that the platform is not what moves Me. It is the intimate worship of My children as they engage My Presence. I desire face time with you, time with you laid upon My altar, surrendering all. Lay your gifts on the altar. The greatest prophetic revelations will be in the secret place with Me. The greatest audience you will ever have is Me. Your place is around My throne to be known by Me. If you desire man and ambition, you may be known on earth, but that does not mean I will know you. Make knowing Me your greatest desire and ambition."
Journal Entry January 24, 2015

PSALM 16:5–8,11, MATTHEW 6:6

PRAYER:
My God, to worship You is the high call. I live to worship You and to glorify You. My gaze is set on You, Jesus. Every gifting and talent in my life is from You, and it is all to be used for the glory of Your Kingdom. Intensify the desire within me to press forward in Your perfect will while maintaining a pure heart with pure motives. There is no greater calling than to worship You and to know You, LORD.

I hear Him saying,

_____

_____

_____

_____

_____

_____

_____

_____

_____

_____

_____

_____

_____

_____

Day 25

Giving It All To Him

I hear Him say, "Am I not a jealous God? Why give parts of yourself away to other things when you can give all of yourself to Me? I do not want pieces of you. I want all of you. I want the fullness of you so that My fullness can abide completely in you and through you. Fullness cannot abide in partial surrender. I have given all of Myself to you. How much of me do you desire?"
Journal Entry August 5, 2016

LUKE 9:23-25, COLOSSIANS 2:9-15

PRAYER:
Jesus, I am most complete when I give all of myself to You. So many things vie for my attention. I desire to have every aspect of my life lived to honor and glorify You, LORD. I will not give in to distractions that cause me to only give you pieces of myself. Your fullness dwells bodily, not partially. I give my all to You, God. I refuse to give You anything less than everything.

I hear Him saying,

_____

_____

_____

_____

_____

_____

_____

_____

_____

_____

_____

_____

_____

_____

_____

Day 26

Fresh Breath In His Garden

I hear Him say, "I am blowing dust off of dry bones, and I am raging once again through dry river beds. I am removing the weeds from My garden. You are My garden and life is found in you as you dwell in the secret place. This is where our love blooms and never fades. My Living water supplies all you need. As you drink in My Presence, and I overcome the dry places with My breath, our love will blossom as your fragrance sails on the wind and into My heart."
Journal Entry August 2, 2015

SONG OF SOLOMON 4:12-16, GENESIS 2:7-8

PRAYER:
I am Your garden, Jesus. You have desired a garden from the beginning and intimacy without end. Holy Spirit, breathe a fresh breath over Your garden, and flood the dry places with Your Living water. Strip out every weed and their root systems. Let this life be fertile ground for You to cultivate a habitation that is fragrant and pleasing to You.

I hear Him saying,

_____

_____

_____

_____

_____

_____

_____

_____

_____

_____

_____

_____

_____

_____

_____

_____

Day 27

Dancing With God

I spent time today worshipping without music, receiving communion, and soaking in His Presence. As I stretched out my arms in worship, My Father lifted me as if I were a small child reaching up to Him. He took me in His arms, and we began to dance. I got lost in His Presence. With each passing day, I love Him more. He is my everything. I want Him to be my obsession. It is difficult at times. There is so much I want to surrender to Him. My flesh is weak, but my spirit is willing. To give Him everything, that is the cry of my heart. I do not want to leave His Presence. He is precious to me.
Journal Entry January 28, 2013

PSALM 30:11–12, JEREMIAH 29:11–13

PRAYER:
Abba, I love spending time in Your Presence and getting to know You more. You are a good Father. You are a faithful Bridegroom, Jesus. I want to dance with You and draw closer to You every single day. I choose to respond when You call me to forsake all else to come away with You. I make You my priority because spending time alone with You is priceless.

I hear Him saying,

_____

_____

_____

_____

_____

_____

_____

_____

_____

_____

_____

_____

_____

_____

_____

_____

_____

Day 28

Show Me Your Glory

I hear Him say, "I have come like I promised. There will be those who turn their faces from Me, even those who have proclaimed out of unrenewed hearts and minds that they will follow Me. Their mouths say the right things, but their hearts are far from Me. They will turn their faces from Me. But those who turn their faces toward Me, their faces will radiate My glory. The temple will overflow with My radiance and My glory. My love will unleash from My bride. The way has been prepared for My glory to explode onto My people and through My people. Now is the time to cry out with desperation unto Me. I have come like I promised and this is only the beginning.

Journal Entry March 28, 2013

EXODUS 33:17–19, 34:29, MATTHEW 7:7–8

PRAYER:

There is no veil to separate us, LORD. I am thankful to have full access to speak face to face with You. Show me Your glory, God. I want to take in the majesty of Your splendor and Your beauty. Let Your glory rest upon my life in such a way that it radiates before others. I do not want religion. I want You. Renew my heart and my mind with Your Word and Your Presence. Mold me as I come into Your glory. I desire Your inner work to manifest outwardly in my life.

I hear Him saying,

_____

_____

_____

_____

_____

_____

_____

_____

_____

_____

_____

_____

_____

_____

_____

_____

Day 29

I Am Your Child

I hear Him say, "I want you to be My daughter first. Your calling I have given you is second. Sons and daughters do what their Father is doing. Your birthright is found in doing and being like Me, not who you think you should be, or who others want you to be. You are My child first. The calling is second. Do what I would do with My heart, and the calling will follow My order. Do not faint or lose heart. No matter how lonely you may feel, I am always with you. Speak My heart and My truth, and you will never go wrong when you follow Me."

Journal Entry June 10, 2013

ISAIAH 43:1,6–7, ROMANS 8:14–16

PRAYER:
Abba, my identity is first found in You. I am Your child, and I walk in Your ways and receive what Jesus did on the cross for my redemption. I rest in Your Presence, knowing that my worth and value is first found in knowing You. I refuse to be restless about my calling. Forgive me for times when I have made the calling bigger than my identity in You. I am completely Yours. My joy is found in You, God.

I hear Him saying,

Day 30

A Lover Of His Presence

I hear Him say, "What is a lover? A lover is fully immersed in My very being. A lover is infatuated with Me, past obsession to the pinnacle of absolute desperation. There is no distinction between the two of us. The beginning cannot be separated from the end. The depth of affection is immeasurable. The gauge of loyalty is incalculable. As I engulf you in My waves of love, we become one and you are lost and found all at once."

Journal Entry August 2, 2014

PSALM 42:1-2, PSALM 26:8, PSALM 41:12

PRAYER:
My God, I love Your Presence. In Your Presence, I am forever transformed. I am desperate for You, Jesus. Let desire overtake me for You in moments of the day as I seek You in the secret place. I want to pour out my love for You and only You. Consume me with passion for Your ways and Your Presence. Interrupt my day to share Your heart with me. I want to get lost in Your glory and Your beauty. Your Presence is everything to me, Lord.

I hear Him saying,

_____

_____

_____

_____

_____

_____

_____

_____

_____

_____

_____

_____

_____

_____

_____

_____

_____

Day 31

Deep Calls Unto Deep

The deeper we go, the more that is revealed about God. The deeper we go, the more unknown facets become known to us about His Presence. I heard Him say, "The deep is not for the timid. It is for those who are fearless and ready to inhabit the secret place, that place reserved for peculiar people. The deep is not a place to hide, but it is a place to shine with a radiance of My Presence not seen in the shallow waters." It is a choice to go to the deep. Deep cries out to deep. We were made for the depths of God. He cries out to the part of us that resounds the crashing waves of His glory. Plunging into the deep will be the portal to His glory, revival of His bride, and a passion that cannot be quenched.
Journal Entry January 5, 2014

PSALM 42:7-8, SONG OF SOLOMON 8:6-7

PRAYER:
I hear You calling to the depths of Yourself within me, God, and I choose to answer Your call. You are calling me to come out of my comfort zone and into uncharted waters in Your Presence. I am diving to the deep because I want You. I was made for the deep. I will not stand in the shallows any longer. I am going where You are, and You are in the deep.

I hear Him saying,

Day 32

Perfect In Weakness

I hear Him say, "Every weakness you have I count as strength because it is in weakness that I shine. I am pleased when a heart lays bare before Me. Imperfection draws Me to you because a vessel willing to reveal its cracks and flaws will allow the process of refinement. I am not looking for perfect people, perfect by their own standards. No, I am looking for those who cry out to search them and to test them. I am looking for those who will bend their will to Mine. I am looking for a people of faith and fidelity. I am looking for a people to consume and to commune with, a people who have my vision and run with it, fanning the flame of Heaven wherever they go."
Journal Entry October 11, 2013

2 CORINTHIANS 12:9–10, EPHESIANS 3:14–21

PRAYER:
Father, nothing is hidden from Your sight. You see every part of me, and You love me. Search me, LORD. Reveal to me the areas needing refining and mending. My strength comes from You. Jesus, I lay every weakness and every shortcoming at Your feet. Holy Spirit, renew my mind and strengthen my inner being. I choose to be vulnerable before You because I want to be the masterpiece You commissioned before the foundations of the earth.

I hear Him saying,

_____

_____

_____

_____

_____

_____

_____

_____

_____

_____

_____

_____

_____

_____

_____

Day 33

The Lord's Catapult

The LORD began to move on me this morning as I spent time with Him. I saw a vision of a catapult in my spirit. It was a simple wooden catapult with a base and legs. Ropes were attached to the legs and dangling between the ropes was a large cup. The base of the catapult represented the Word of God. The legs represented worship. The ropes represented fasting and prayer, and the cup was the cup of surrender. I heard Him say, "If you will submit yourself to My Word, prayer, fasting, and worship, and if you will willingly lay down in the place of surrender, I will launch you out at the right time."
Journal Entry April 26, 2016

ECCLESIASTES 3:11, PROVERBS 3:5–6

PRAYER:
I trust Your timing and Your ways, God. I love Your Word, and I love to worship and to praise Your Holy Name in every area of my life. Stir up a hunger and a passion to fervently pray and to crucify my flesh with fasting. I lay myself down in the cup of surrender, and I wait for You, LORD. I remain in Your process, knowing that Your ways are higher than mine, and Your timing is right on time. I choose a lifestyle submitted fully to You, even after You launch me out for Your glory.

I hear Him saying,

_____

_____

_____

_____

_____

_____

_____

_____

_____

_____

_____

_____

_____

_____

_____

Day 34

Soften My Heart, Jesus

I hear Him say, "I desire for My ocean of anointing to dash the hearts of stone. Hardened hearts cannot receive My anointing. They hear the waves pounding on them, but they refuse to be undone. They feel the shaking from My glory, but they say nothing will move them. But I hear the cry from within those who want to come out into the deep. I will flood them with My Presence. I will consume them in My glory. My breath will flow through the ocean of My anointing. Things buried in the deep will be uncovered and brought to the surface, and My majesty will be manifested on the face of the deep. Age is of no consideration to me. I simply desire willing hearts and yielded vessels."
Journal Entry April 2, 2013

EZEKIEL 36:26–27, 2 CORINTHIANS 3:3

PRAYER:
Jesus, soften my heart, and write Your Word upon my heart. I yield myself to You in every area of my life. I want to move with You and go where You are going. Instill in me a passion for Your Word. I repent of stubbornness and diminished desire for Your Presence and Your Truth. Blow through me, Holy Spirit. Stir up the Living waters on the inside of me, and dash them against the stony portions of my heart so that it can truly beat for You without limits.

I hear Him saying,

_____

_____

_____

_____

_____

_____

_____

_____

_____

_____

_____

_____

_____

_____

_____

_____

_____

Day 35

The Royal Priesthood

I hear Him say, "You are the fiery stones on My holy mountain. You are My tents that go with the cloud of glory before you and the pillar of fire surrounding you. The precious Blood is painted over the doorposts to your heart. You are My priesthood, adorned with garments of holiness, and you come before Me to intercede for the generations and the nations. You come with unveiled faces because you have full access, and when you come, you make deposits with live coals on My altar. You are to carry my glory, and you are never to be stationary, but always moving and flowing with the ebbs of My Presence."
Journal Entry August 25, 2015

1 PETER 2:9–10, DEUTERONOMY 7:6

PRAYER:
Father, stir the passion within me for intercession and prayer. I am part of the royal priesthood, and I want to pray the prayers that You are praying, Jesus. Let my prayers reach Your throne room and align with the plans and the purposes of Heaven. I want to be a vessel of glory for You. I desire to overflow with Your Presence in such a way that those around me are transformed by Your power and Your glory. Remind me every day that I belong to You.

I hear Him saying,

_____

_____

_____

_____

_____

_____

_____

_____

_____

_____

_____

_____

_____

_____

_____

_____

Day 36

A Hunger For His Word

I saw a vision this morning of a cloud. It was full of thunder and lightning, and it was moving in on the winds. I saw saints of God falling to their knees because of the weight of glory coming down. I saw a mighty downpour from this cloud, and the Word was in the downpour, falling to the ground. I watched as hungry people began to eat the Word, and thirsty people gulped down water from the rivers released from the cloud of glory. I heard Him say, "Just like natural food changes the structure and function of the body, so does My Word and My rivers of Living water. What you consume, you become."
Journal Entry August 23, 2015

JOSHUA 1:8, JOHN 6:48–58

PRAYER:
Jesus, You are the Bread of life. You spoke to the thirsty, and you gave an invitation to come and drink. Holy Spirit, You are the Living water. Stir hunger in me for Your Word and Your Presence. Let it be a hunger and a thirst that remains with me every moment of every day. Illuminate Your Word when I read it, and speak to me as I digest Your truth and drink in Your Presence. Do a deep work within me, and help me to transform my spiritual diet.

I hear Him saying,

Day 37

The Call To Repentance

I hear Him say, "Repentance must come to My bride before it can come to the world. The cry in this hour must be a cry of forgiveness, humility, and repentance from My bride. When this happens, coals will be heaped upon the powers of darkness, and the fire from the altar will go forth to change a nation and a generation. My Presence is found in repentance. It is a level of intimacy drawing Me to My bride. Repentance and fervent prayer are the thunders I wish to release upon those who will bend to My will."
Journal Entry July 5, 2015

ISAIAH 44:22, ACTS 3:19–21

PRAYER:
Jesus, let repentance be found on my lips when I miss the mark and fall short of Your glory. Convict my heart of things that grieve You, and renew a right spirit in me. I want to draw closer to You. I choose You, my First Love. I choose a life worthy of the calling You set before me. There is no condemnation in You, Jesus. Your kindness leads me to repentance. Let everything I do in this life be with You in mind, to be holy as You are holy.

I hear Him saying,

_____

_____

_____

_____

_____

_____

_____

_____

_____

_____

_____

_____

_____

_____

_____

_____

_____

Day 38

I'm Letting Go

This morning, I heard You speaking to me as I sought You. I have sensed a transition coming, the end of one season to prepare for the next. I heard You say as I asked for direction, "Come sit at My feet. It is the time to be Mary and not Martha. Come glean from My Word." My heart says, "Yes", and my spirit says, "I will worship you anywhere, no matter where I am or how I am positioned. I will worship You." I heard you say, "Let go. In order to grasp what waits for you in this next season, you must let go of what you hold onto now." *Journal Entry August 22, 2015*

LUKE 10:38–42, PHILIPPIANS 3:13–16

PRAYER:
God, I choose the better portion that is You. I refuse to live a life where I do not make time for communion with You. I will sit at Your feet and spend time with You as You share Your heart with me in the secret place. I will choose Your ways when You are leading me down a new path and into a new season. Help me to be sensitive when grace lifts from a season, and find me obedient to Your will. Wherever You are is where I want to be, Jesus. Your perfect will is the best destination.

I hear Him saying,

_____

_____

_____

_____

_____

_____

_____

_____

_____

_____

_____

_____

_____

_____

_____

Day 39

I Am His Incense

I hear Him say, "You are My incense. I want your life to permeate a pleasing fragrance. As you lay on the altar of sacrifice and permit Me to burn through you with My fire and My Spirit, I will be pleased with the aroma from your life. You were always meant to dwell in My secret place. Incense must burn before an aroma is released. Your life is meant to be infused with the fragrance of Heaven. Every life permeates and emits a fragrance. Some smell of death, some smell of life. Then there are those who have bowed down at My feet, and their death to self has created such an aroma that it intoxicates My throne. Let your life produce a weighty fragrance unto Me. Permit the coals to touch you, and as they do, the aroma of Heaven will be released. You were always meant to dwell in My Presence, My burnished bride.
Journal Entry June 18, 2013

JOHN 12:1–3, 2 CORINTHIANS 2:14–16

PRAYER:
Father, I want my life to be a pleasing aroma before Your throne. Let Your fire consume me, and let this life release the fragrance of Christ. Let those around me smell Your fragrance, and let it be contagious to those I come in contact. You deserve all the glory, God. I want to dwell with You in the secret place, the fragrant place.

I hear Him saying,

_____

_____

_____

_____

_____

_____

_____

_____

_____

_____

_____

_____

_____

_____

_____

Day 40

All I Want Is You

"All I want is You. Keep me here with You, Lord. Even if it is the wilderness, keep me here with You. Strip me clean of all that keeps me from the fullness of Your Presence. Over and over, You confirm the season I am entering. So, I welcome it because it is Your will. I thank You for pruning me, for cleansing me, and for preparing me. Holy Spirit, I yield myself to You. I give myself over to You. Whether I am hidden from people or I am in full view, I only want You, and when I stand before man, let Your light shine through me. Let them see You. I give all the glory to You. I am in love with You, My Jesus." *Journal Entry April 7, 2013*

PSALM 73:25–26, PHILIPPIANS 3:8

PRAYER:
There are no words to fully describe what You mean to me, Jesus. Nothing compares to Your Presence. Nothing is sweeter than Your love. No one loves me like You do, LORD. You are my one desire. I am desperate for You. This journey does not end here at day forty. This is only the beginning of a great romance with the Lover of my soul. You have captured my heart, and I will spend every day in full pursuit of You.

I hear Him saying,

Communion

And when he had given thanks, he broke it, and said, "This is my body which is for you. Do this in remembrance of me." In the same way also he took the cup, after supper, saying, "This cup is the new covenant in my blood. Do this, as often as you drink it, in remembrance of me." For as often as you eat this bread and drink the cup, you proclaim the Lord's death until he comes. 1 Corinthians 11:24-26

Receiving communion is not reserved to a corporate gathering or a special occasion. As the bride of Christ, communion is an intimate aspect of our personal relationship with Christ, and it is something we can receive in our private times with the Lord.

It may surprise you to know that the cup we receive for communion is the third cup received during the Passover feast. It is known as the cup of redemption. This is the same cup Jesus receives in Matthew 26:26-28 and Luke 22:19-20. The cup of redemption is also referred to as the cup of betrothal, which correlates to the Jewish wedding custom of a man offering a cup of wine to a prospective bride during a wedding proposal. The acceptance of the betrothal was found in the woman drinking the cup. When we receive communion, we are saying yes to the Lord's proposal to be His bride, and every time we receive communion, we renew that commitment to our Bridegroom!

Based on this alone, you can see why communion is such an important part of our relationship with Christ, and the wonderful opportunity we have as believers to receive it. Not only do we renew our covenant to Christ, but we also call to remembrance His sacrifice and His atonement for us to be reconciled to God in every aspect of our lives. God desires for us to be whole physically, mentally, and emotionally, nothing missing and nothing broken.

When you receive communion:

- Expect the manifest Presence of God during this intimate moment
- Examine yourself and discern your body according to the Word of God (1 Corinthians 11:24-25) before receiving communion. Repent of anything not pleasing to the Lord, and receive His forgiveness.
- If you need healing in your body or your mind, communion is a powerful element to receive along with prayer and meditating on the Word of God.
- Prayer is simply talking to God. Take time to pray during this time. Simple prayers are just as powerful as eloquent prayers.
- Worship the Lord after you receive communion, and give Him praise. He is worthy of our adoration!

With regards to the elements for communion, consider using crackers for the body, though bread is fine. Regular grape juice is perfect for receiving the cup to drink.

I encourage you to meditate on these Scriptures when receiving communion: Matthew 26:26-28, Luke 22:19-20, and 1 Corinthians 11:23-24, 28-29. You may find it easier to use these Scriptures in the beginning to serve yourself each element of communion as you pray. Follow the leading of the Holy Spirit while being in unity with the Word of God as you renew your covenant with the Lord during the next 40 days of intimate pursuit.

Refuse to allow this opportunity to become a religious act. Anything done repetitively can become legalistic. Communion with our Lord is a beautiful thing. Let's keep it intimate and focused on relationship with our Bridegroom!

About the Author

Dawn Hill is a prophetic voice and writer known as the Lovesick Scribe. Her ministry focuses on passionately pursuing the Bridegroom while encouraging others to do the same. She serves at Impact HUB in Bristol, Virginia, training and equipping fellow believers to hear the voice of God and to function in the gift of prophecy. She resides in Virginia with her husband and her daughter.

Subscribe to Dawn Hill's blog, Lovesick Scribe at

www.lovesickscribe.com

Made in the USA
Middletown, DE
04 June 2017